Introduction

Much like a mandala, the animal kingdom is intricately detailed, with a wide variety of shapes, patterns, and elements to discover. From the tiniest leaf in a forest to the most miniscule swirl in a mandala, each factor is intrinsically important to the result as a whole. Without the leaf, the insect would go hungry. Without the insect, the frog would have no food. If there were no small swirls in a mandala, it would not have the same effect, would not have the same meditative, Zen-like qualities. In both mandalas and the animal kingdom, every little piece counts. Every shape and line and flower is exactly where it is meant to be.

As you color these mandalas based on the animal kingdom, let your mind find peace in the repetitious movement of the art. Let the quotes about each little part of the animal kingdom guide you to a feeling of wholeness, of a fullness of mind and spirit. Take your time and let your markers, pencils, or crayons guide you to where you should color next. Explore the animal kingdom in a way that many never discover: meditatively.

The next few pages have a colored art gallery so your inspiration can take flight. There is also a gallery in the very back to encourage your creativity and to give you a jumping-off point. So, as you wander through the animal kingdom by way of the mandala, be sure to keep your mind open, your spirit free, and your pencil sharpened. Enjoy!

WHAT IS A MANDALA?

"Mandala" is a word that means "circle" or "center" in Sanskrit. Mandalas are seen as a meditation aid to guide one through their spiritual journey in the Hindu and Buddhist traditions, although mandalas are seen throughout many cultures. As you will notice in this book, each mandala is designed to create a meditative art experience, using intricate, circu[...] designs with animals, leaves, flowers, and so much more. As you color each mandala, focus on the process, and let your mind relax. Drawing and coloring mandalas are great ways to relieve stress and work on your mindfulness.

Supplies

If you're just starting your coloring adventure, get ready for a whole new world of discovery! From markers and colored pencils to gel pens and pastels, today's coloring supplies offer colorists plenty of opportunities to play, experiment, and create stunning works of art. You can find basic coloring supplies at almost any store, which makes it convenient to get started.

Coloring supplies can range in price from economical to artist-quality expensive. While a higher price point often yields higher quality, if you're just getting started and you're on a budget, don't get too hung up on brands. Instead, experiment with whatever supplies you can afford as you practice coloring the designs in this book. When you use the right techniques, even the cheapest coloring supplies can yield dazzling works of art! Then, when you're ready, you can add more expensive brands to your cache of supplies.

Colored Pencils

Colored pencils are an attractive choice for coloring because they can be used to achieve vibrant blends, subtle shading, and beautiful details, and they also tend to be more forgiving than markers and other mediums. While it typically takes longer to color with colored pencils than it does with markers, the luminous results can make the effort totally worth it! There are plenty of colored pencil options on the market, and it all comes down to what feels right for you. Here are some things to think about when you set out to purchase colored pencils.

Many colored pencil brands offer two different types of pencils: inexpensive student-quality pencils and artist-quality (also called professional-quality) pencils that cost more but contain higher pigment content, resulting in richer, more vivid colors. If you decide to purchase artist-quality colored pencils, your next consideration will be whether to get oil-based pencils or wax-based pencils. Student-quality pencils are typically only wax-based. Before you purchase your colored pencils, be sure to check the label to see whether they are student-grade or artist-grade, because there can be a noticeable difference in quality and user experience.

When you use colored pencils, you can easily achieve vibrant results that seamlessly blend together.

> ## TIP
> A kneaded eraser is a good choice when trying to erase colored pencil.

Markers

The markers most commonly used for coloring are either alcohol-based or water-based. (Oil-based markers are geared toward surfaces other than paper.) Water-based marker colors can be diluted with water, while alcohol-based markers can be blended by layering colors or using rubbing alcohol. (A colorless blender marker will help you achieve results with both types of marker.) One advantage to using alcohol-based markers is that they will not warp or buckle thinner paper the way water-based markers do.

Dual-tip markers, like these water-based brush markers from Tombow, give you a lot of flexibility and control in a single marker.

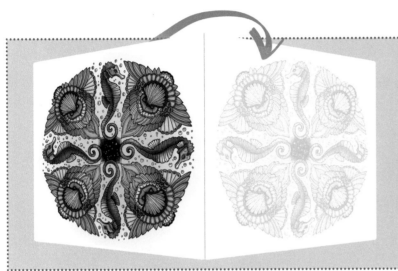

TIP

Markers sometimes bleed through your coloring pages. One trick to help with this is to put a scrap page underneath your design, which will catch any bleed-through and prevent it from getting onto other coloring pages or your table. Another trick is to spray hairspray or another fixative onto your blank page before you color it with markers. This will minimize marker bleed-through . . . but test it on a sample page first!

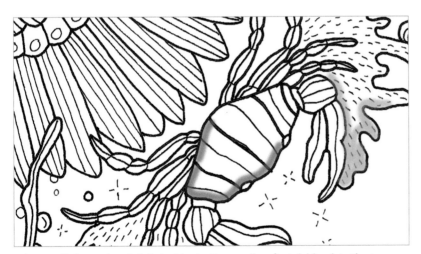

When outlining, color slightly inside the line to allow for ink bleed. In the image above, the blue in the center was colored not quite up to the black line, and the color bled up to the line nicely. The red edge was colored right up to the black line, and bled over it.

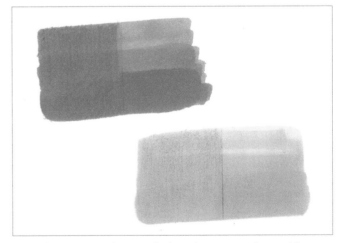

Smooth out any marker streaks by coloring over them with a matching colored pencil. The left sides were colored over with colored pencil.

Gel Pens

Gel pens are perfect for enhancing and embellishing colored pieces. Because they are pens with fine-tip points, coloring an entire page with them would be very time-consuming; however, gel pens can be used to accentuate smaller areas in many unique and fun ways. Because of their unique ink, gel pens produce colors with a different tone and quality than markers and colored pencils. Try using them to add little pops of neon or other vibrant colors to a piece you've completed with markers or colored pencils.

Blue metallic on a blue base—not so great.

Gold glitter on a lilac base—it works!

Yellow glaze pen on an orange base—doesn't work.

Use slow, steady strokes to avoid line skipping.

TIP

Gel pens are awesome detailers because they are opaque in nature, but they do require a little bit of experimentation; some tones will not show up well when layered on top of dark base shades.

Allow time for the ink to dry to avoid smears—try working in the direction of your dominant hand (if you're right-handed, from left to right).

Crayons

Pretty much everyone can remember coloring when they were younger with a good old box of crayons. After all, they are the quintessential children's coloring tool. Unfortunately, they're not generally suited for creating polished, professional-looking pieces.

The good thing about crayons is that they are incredibly affordable and they come in a massive range of colors for very little investment. You can also get crayons that come in pencil form now, such as Crayola Twistables®. Some adults find coloring with traditional crayons either childish or difficult (due to the short length of the crayons), so these pencil-like crayons can help with that.

Overall, for a beginning colorist or someone who just likes the nostalgia of coloring with crayons, they can be a good investment. Just don't expect polished results without quite a bit of effort.

Crayons have their own unique textured effect.

Watercolors

There are many different techniques for using watercolors. You can use a lot of water and a little bit of color to make a pretty, ethereal wash of color on an entire page or a large section of a design, and then color or create a pattern on top of that. You can also use very little water for a drybrush effect, which can create interesting textures and a more vivid color payoff. You can put water on the paper first and then bleed color into it, and you can also do it the other way around, laying down a somewhat dry swath of color and then adding more water to it to blend it out. You can blend your watercolors together to make new colors either directly on the paper or separately on a palette. The possibilities are endless!

WATERCOLOR IN COLORING BOOKS

Because coloring book pages tend to be on the thin side, most won't hold up to more than a little water. To eliminate this problem, copy the coloring page design onto heavier watercolor paper. If you want to use the paper that came in your coloring book, it is best to tear it out of the book to prevent ruining any pages underneath it. Paint a few test swatches on an inconspicuous corner of the paper to see how the paper reacts.

Color Theory

Let's start with the color wheel. This simple tool is the basis for everything you need to know to get started exploring color. I'll use this familiar tool to explain different color categories, relationships, and combinations to help you learn your way around color and color schemes. It's easy for beginners to feel overwhelmed by the sheer volume of colors that their colored pencil or marker sets offer, but a basic understanding of the color wheel and color terminology will help you make use of the thousands of different colors out there.

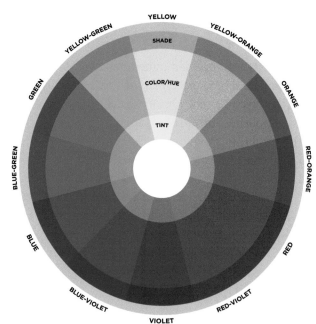

Basic Color Categories

The color wheel can be divided up into many different, helpful "sets" of colors. First, let's explore the most basic.

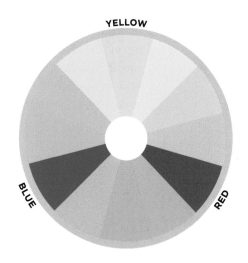

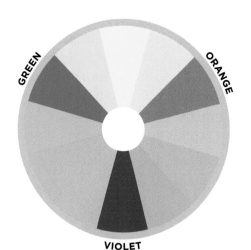

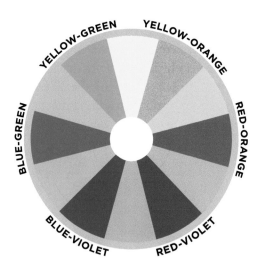

Primary Colors

The three primary colors—red, yellow, and blue—can't be created by mixing any other colors together and are the basis for creating the rest of the colors on the color wheel.

Secondary Colors

The secondary colors are orange, green, and violet (often called purple). They are created by mixing two primary colors together. Mixing the primary colors red and blue creates violet; mixing red and yellow creates orange; mixing blue and yellow creates green.

Tertiary Colors

Tertiary colors are created by mixing a primary (p) color with one of its adjacent secondary (s) colors. For example. mixing red (p) and violet (s) creates the tertiary color red-violet (magenta).

Color Schemes

Now that we've covered the basics of the color wheel, let's talk about color schemes. Color schemes are what we call the combinations of various colors from the color wheel in a piece of artwork. Picking a color scheme from these options is a great way to get started with a piece of art and know that your colors will work well together, but don't be afraid to break away from these models, either. Many great works of art combine all sorts of colors, including all the colors of the rainbow!

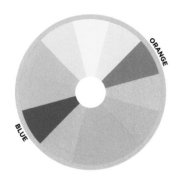 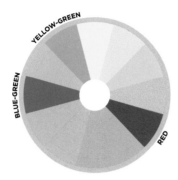 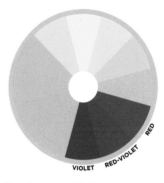 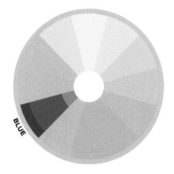

Complementary Colors

Complementary colors are directly opposite each other on the color wheel, such as blue and orange.

Split Complementary Colors

A split complementary color scheme is made up of a color plus the two colors adjacent to its complement. For example, a split complementary scheme might include red, teal (blue-green), and chartreuse (yellow-green).

Analogous Colors

Analogous color schemes use colors that are right next to each other on the color wheel, often in sets of three, and have a very harmonious effect. For instance, violet, magenta (red-violet), and red are analogous.

Monochromatic Colors

If you don't want to think too hard or want to go really simple with your color scheme, try a monochromatic look. Pick a single color, such as blue, and then pull out every blue coloring utensil you have and color with it.

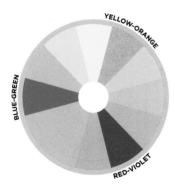 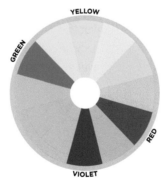 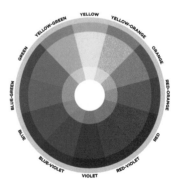

Triadic Colors

If you can imagine an equilateral triangle superimposed on top of the color wheel, the three colors it touches form a triadic color scheme. For example, amber (yellow-orange), magenta (red-violet), and teal (blue-green) are a triad.

Tetradic Colors

Tetradic color schemes are made up of two pairs of complementary colors; imagine a skinny rectangle superimposed on the color wheel. A tetradic color scheme might consist of yellow, violet, red, and green.

Warm and Cool Colors

Warm colors include most red- and yellow-based colors and tend to convey feelings of warmth, energy, and brightness. Cool colors include most blue- and green-based colors and tend to convey feelings of calm, coolness, and depth.

Techniques

Shading

When shading, you need to decide what tools and method you want to use. There are four general methods. The first method—the single-color, two-tool method—creates the most realistic effect.

   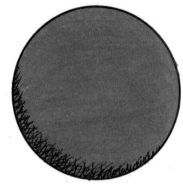

Method 1: Pick two similar shades from the same color family and use them together: a base color (lighter color) and a shade color (darker color).

Method 2: Use varying degrees of pressure with a single coloring tool to make the shaded part darker than the rest.

Method 3: Add black or gray where you want shading, or use a totally different color than the one you're using as a base.

Method 4: Use line techniques like stippling or crosshatching.

Highlighting

A simple way to add highlights to your coloring is to use a white gel pen (for severe highlights) or white colored pencil (for subtle highlights). You could also use a kneaded eraser to pick up some of the base color where you would like to place a highlight; this works best with colored pencils. With a little planning, you can simply leave an area uncolored from the beginning to create a highlight.

 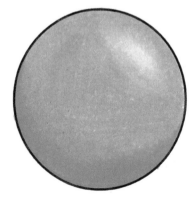 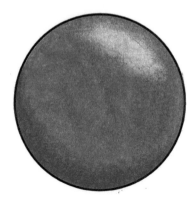

Gel pen highlight

Colored pencil highlight

Highlight created by erasing

Blending

Blending allows you to seamlessly combine colors together to create visually stunning art. When blending, you can use any colors or mediums you want. We recommend starting with a monochromatic color scheme in one specific medium until you get comfortable with the process. Colored pencils are good tools for beginners to learn blending.

TIP

With dry tools, like crayons and colored pencils, tool sharpness and hand pressure make all the difference. With wet tools, these two things are not a factor. Simply layer colors one over another, back and forth.

1. Base

2. Add

3. Blend

Start by laying down the light base color over the entire area you want to blend.

Use the dark shade to color lightly from the middle of the base color toward one edge of the shape. As you move farther away from the area of your base shade, begin adding more pressure to your pencil, coloring the area more heavily.

Go back with the light base color and color over the base and dark shade areas. Repeat until you've created a nice, even coat of color.

BLENDING WITH WET TOOLS

Wet tools, like markers and watercolors, will simply need to be layered over one another, back and forth, to achieve blended colors.

Color by Amanda Fritsch.
Design on page 29.

10

Color by Amanda Fritsch.
Design on page 59.

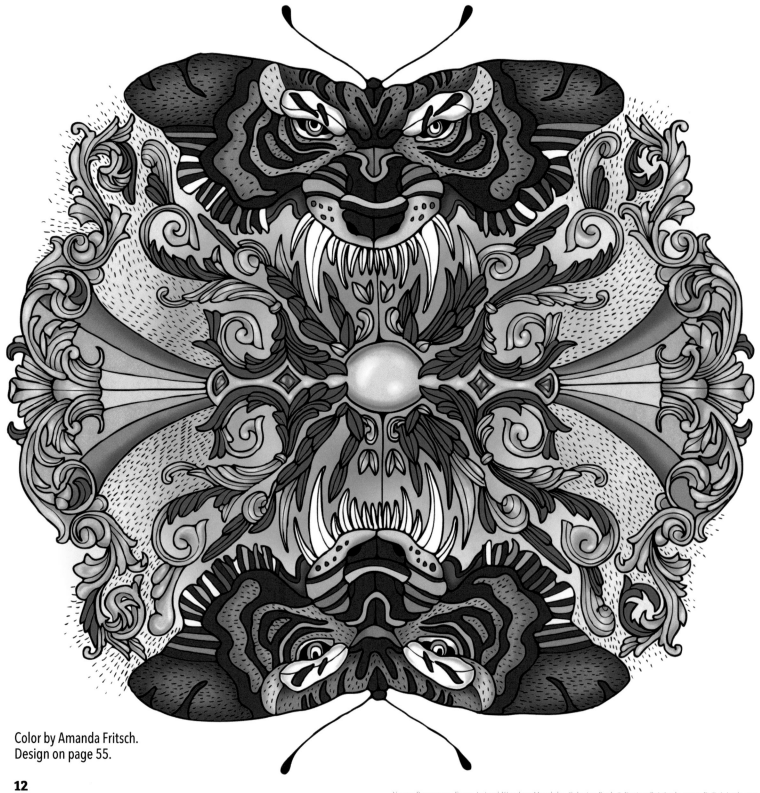

Color by Amanda Fritsch.
Design on page 55.

12

Color by Amanda Fritsch.
Design on page 21.

Color by David Fisk.
Design on page 39.

14

Color by Amanda Fritsch.
Design on page 19.

Color by David Fisk.
Design on page 25.

16

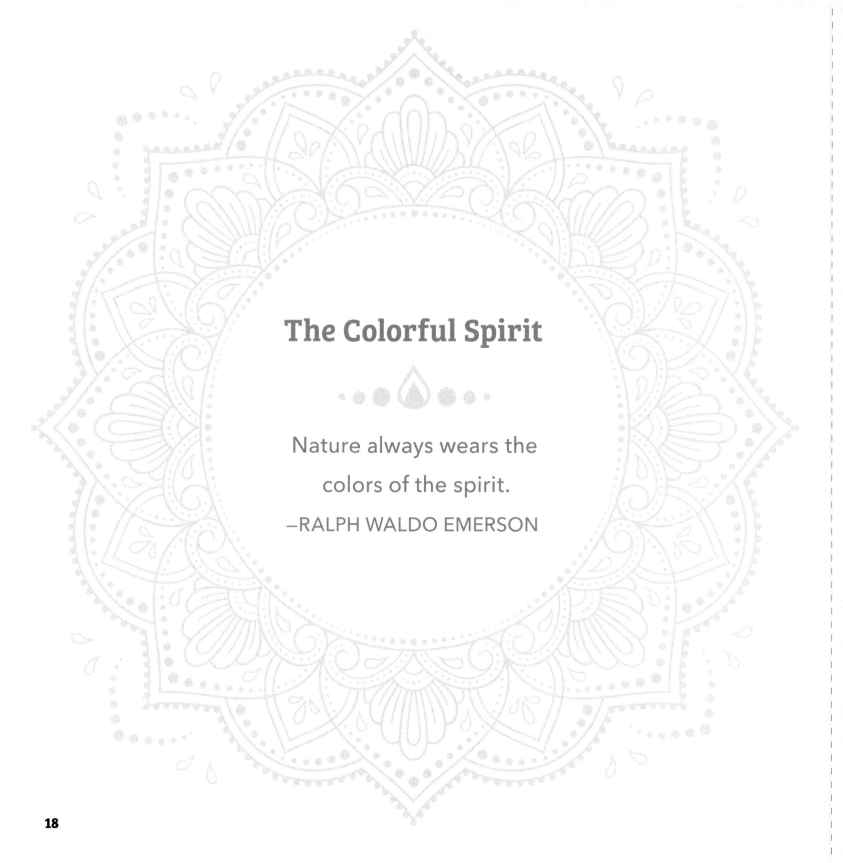

The Colorful Spirit

Nature always wears the
colors of the spirit.

–RALPH WALDO EMERSON

The Woodland Companions

Animals are such agreeable friends—they ask no questions, they pass no criticisms.

–GEORGE ELIOT

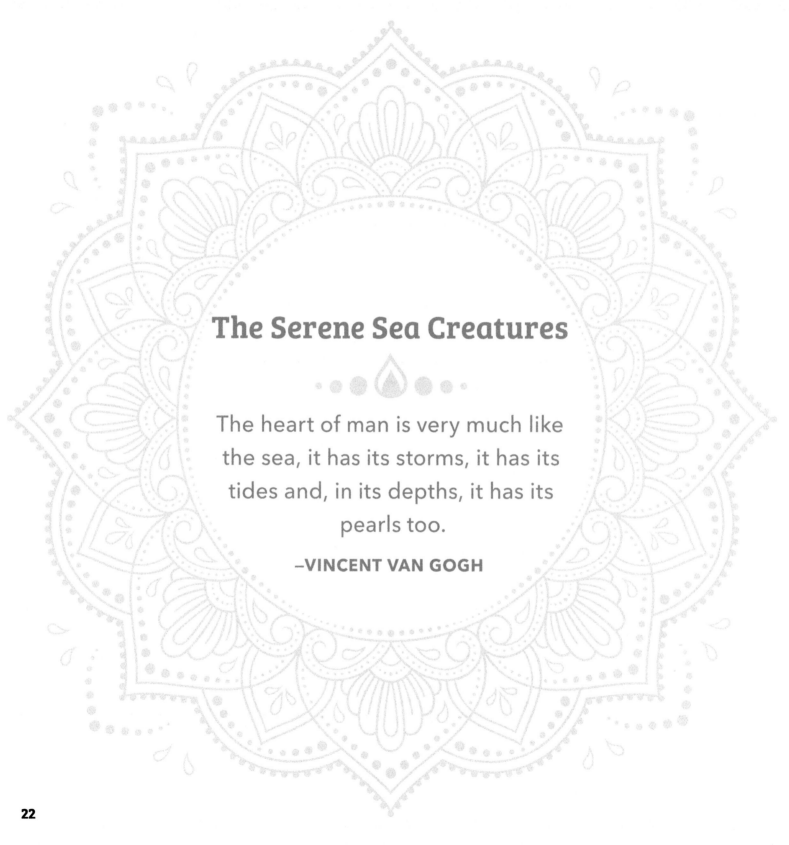

The Serene Sea Creatures

The heart of man is very much like the sea, it has its storms, it has its tides and, in its depths, it has its pearls too.

–VINCENT VAN GOGH

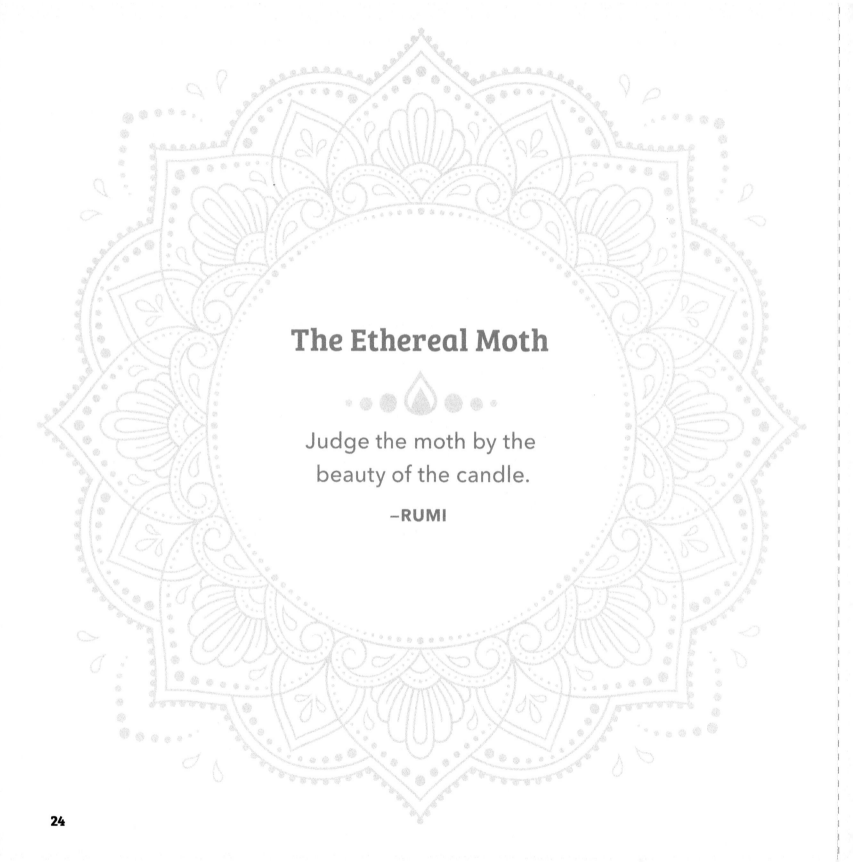

The Ethereal Moth

Judge the moth by the
beauty of the candle.

—RUMI

The Winged Creatures

The higher we soar the smaller
we appear to those who
cannot fly.

–FRIEDRICH NIETZSCHE

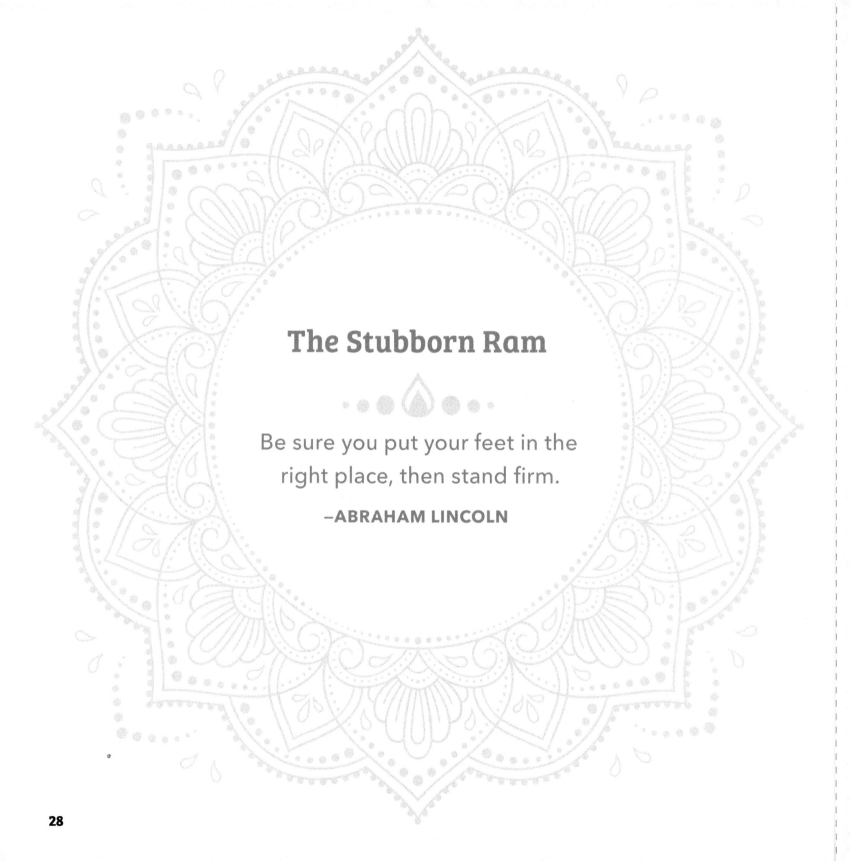

The Stubborn Ram

Be sure you put your feet in the
right place, then stand firm.

–ABRAHAM LINCOLN

The Complex Beetle

An insect is more complex than
a star . . . and is a far greater
challenge to understand.

—MARTIN REES

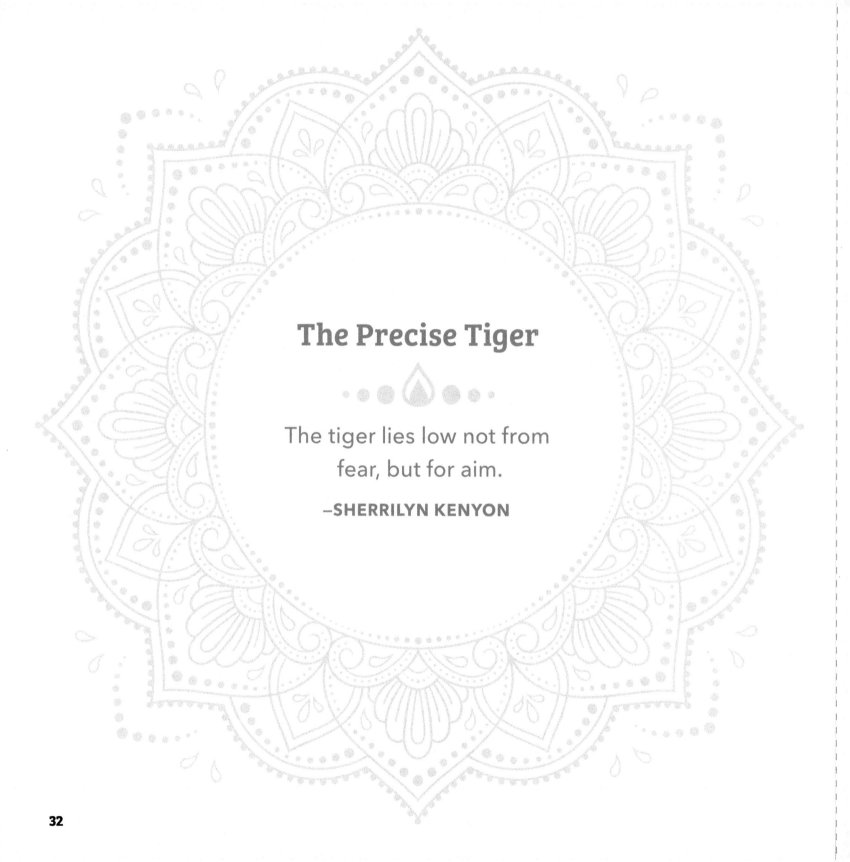

The Precise Tiger

The tiger lies low not from
fear, but for aim.

–SHERRILYN KENYON

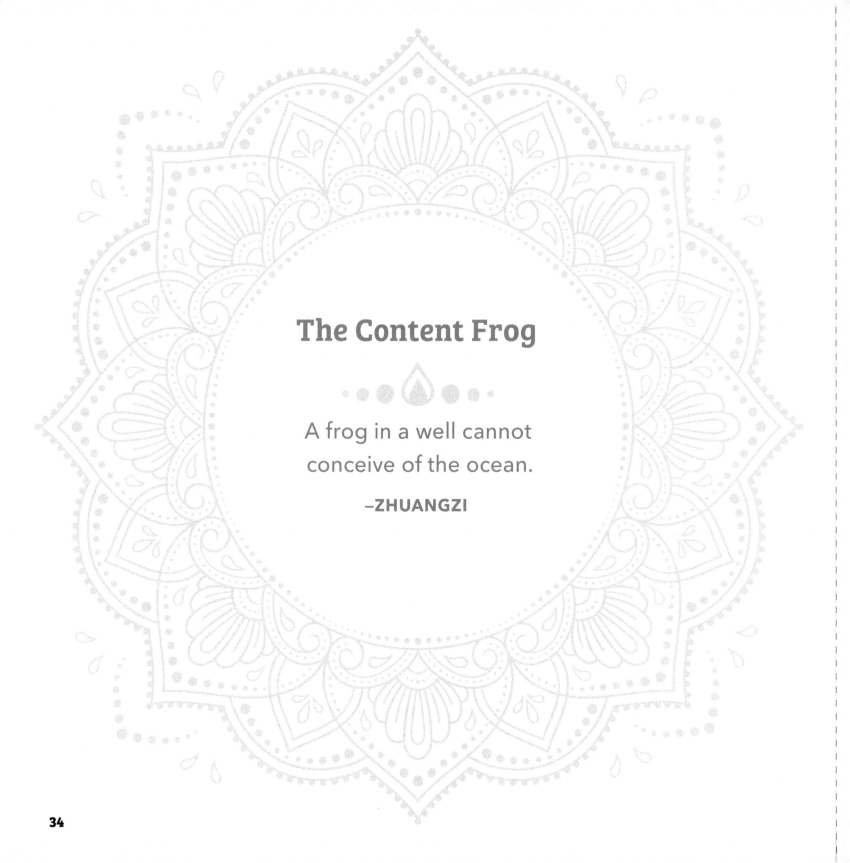

The Content Frog

A frog in a well cannot
conceive of the ocean.

—ZHUANGZI

The Transformed
Butterfly

We delight in the beauty of the butterfly, but rarely admit the changes it has gone through to achieve that beauty.

–MAYA ANGELOU

The Joyful Hummingbird

Like the hummingbird sipping nectar from every flower, I fly joyfully through my days, seeing beauty in everything.

–AMETHYST WYLDFYRE

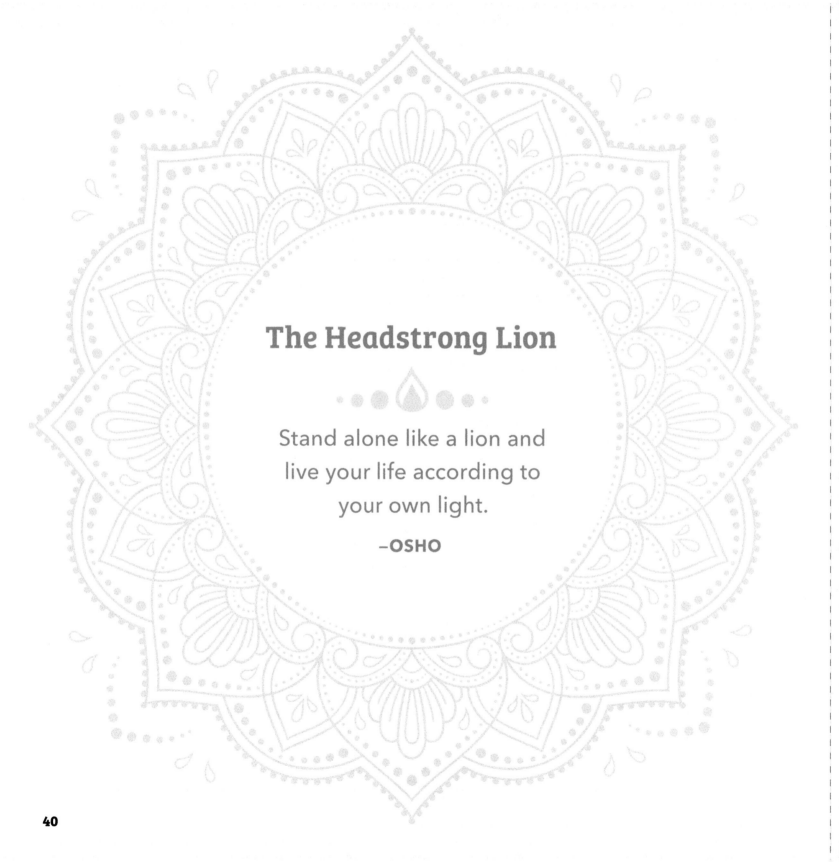

The Headstrong Lion

Stand alone like a lion and
live your life according to
your own light.

–OSHO

The Magnificent Moth

I have a little brown cocoon of an idea that may possibly expand into a magnificent moth of fulfillment.

–LUCY MAUD MONTGOMERY

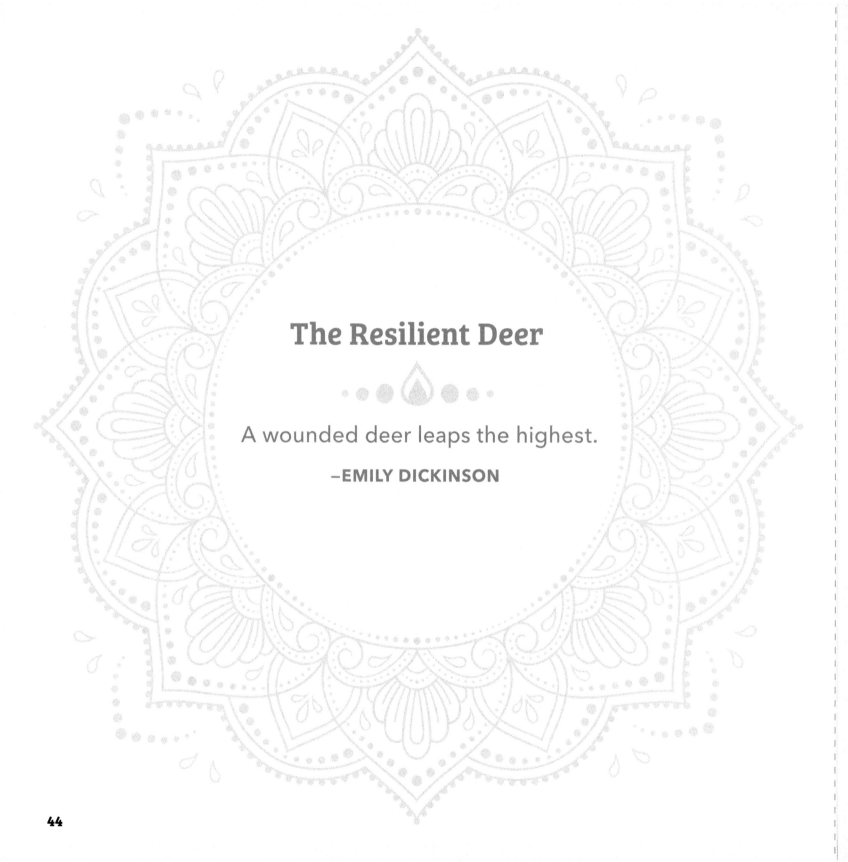

The Resilient Deer

A wounded deer leaps the highest.

–EMILY DICKINSON

The Mindful Fish

Fish don't worry about their fate when you throw them in deep waters.

–MATSHONA DHLIWAYO

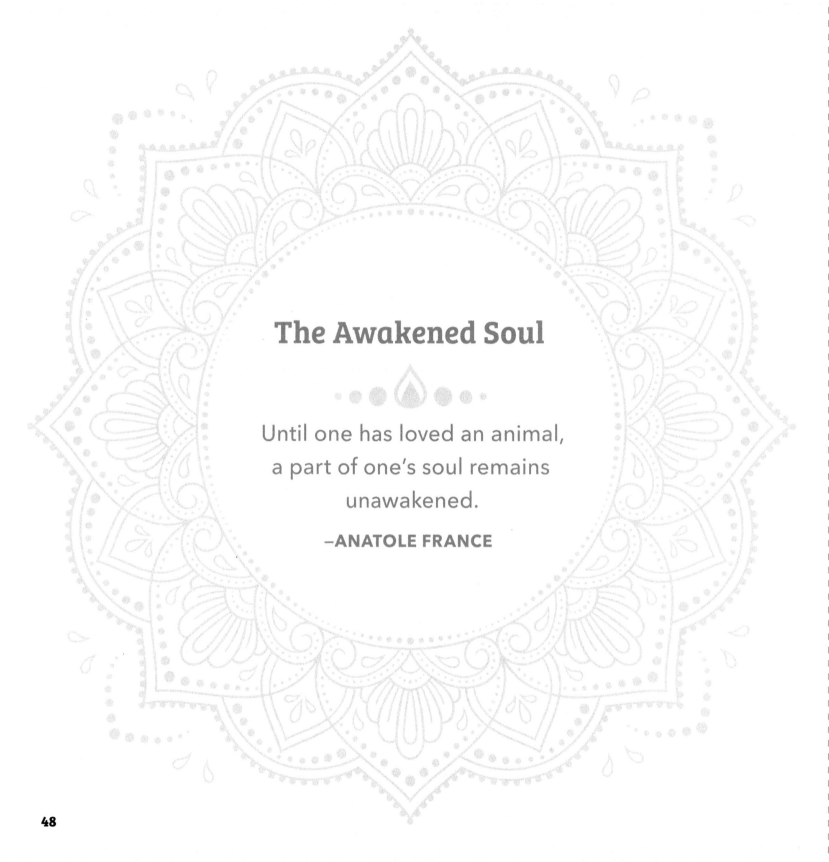

The Awakened Soul

Until one has loved an animal,
a part of one's soul remains
unawakened.

–ANATOLE FRANCE

The Breathtaking Butterfly

If nothing ever changed, there would be no such things as butterflies.

—WENDY MASS

The Contemplative Owl

The Owl thinks slowly,
but the Owl thinks long.

–URSULA K. LE GUIN

The Alert Bear

When you are where
wild bears live, you learn to pay
attention to the rhythm
of the land and yourself.

–LINDA JO HUNTER

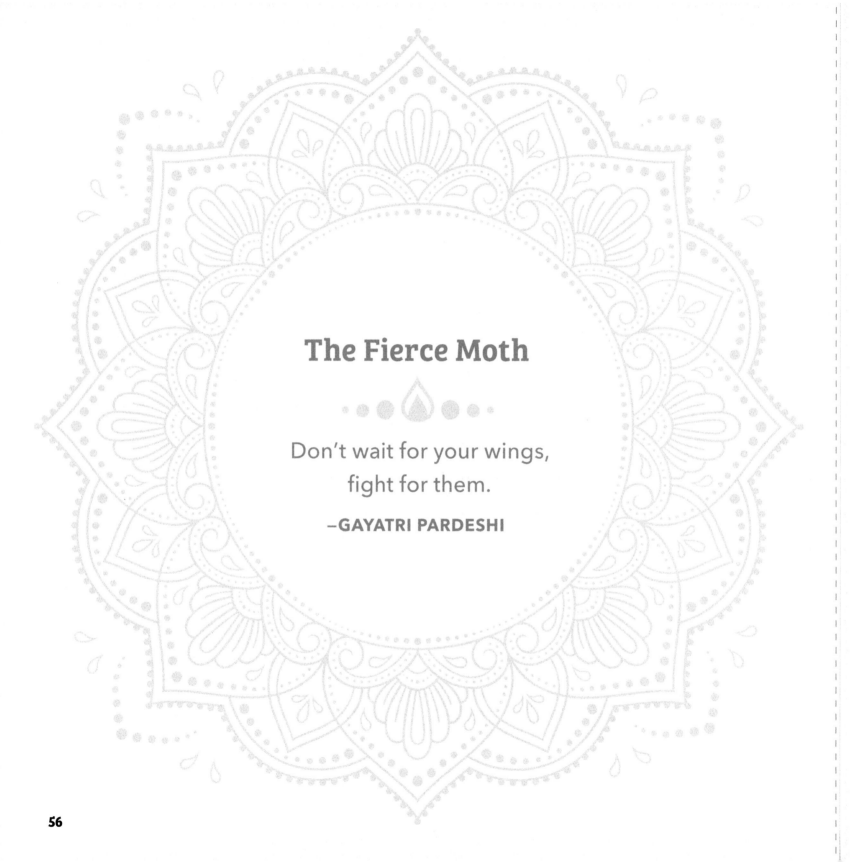

The Fierce Moth

Don't wait for your wings,
fight for them.

—GAYATRI PARDESHI

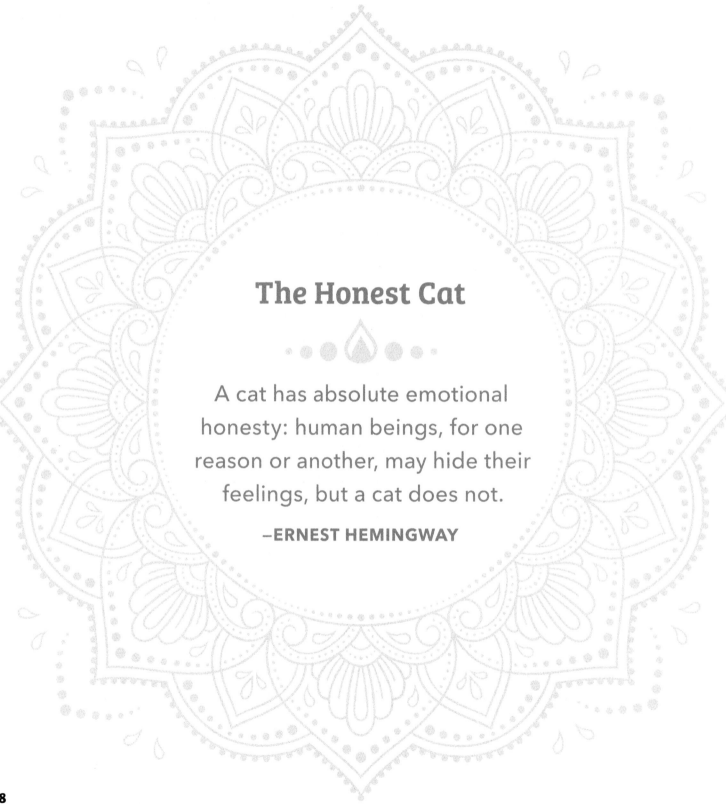

The Honest Cat

A cat has absolute emotional honesty: human beings, for one reason or another, may hide their feelings, but a cat does not.

—ERNEST HEMINGWAY

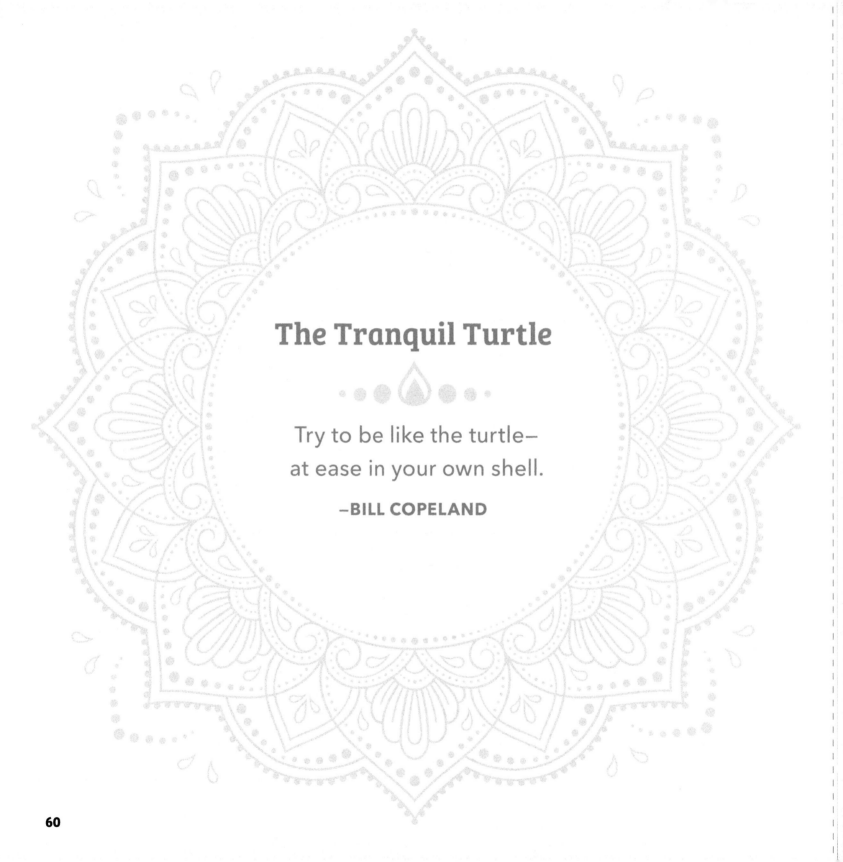

The Tranquil Turtle

Try to be like the turtle—
at ease in your own shell.

–BILL COPELAND

The Busy Bee

The busy bee has no
time for sorrow.

–WILLIAM BLAKE

The Wise Owl

Owls are wise. They are careful and patient. Wisdom precludes boldness. That is why owls make poor heroes.

–PATRICK ROTHFUSS

The Peaceful Jaguar

Animals are born who they are,
accept it, and that is that.
They live with greater peace
than people do.

—GREGORY MAGUIRE

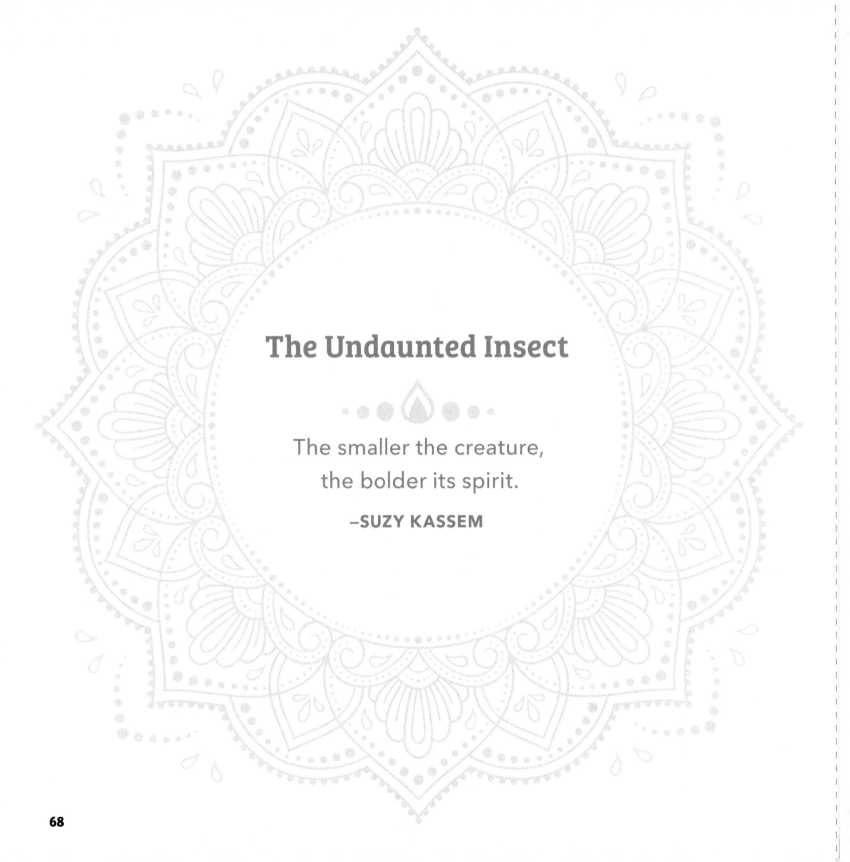

The Undaunted Insect

The smaller the creature,
the bolder its spirit.

–SUZY KASSEM

The Optimistic Bird

Be as a bird perched on a frail
branch that she feels bending
beneath her, still she sings
away all the same,
knowing she has wings.

–VICTOR HUGO

The Gracious Ocean Dwellers

If the ocean can calm itself,
so can you. We are both
saltwater mixed with air.

–NAYYIRAH WAHEED

The Gentle Bee

Hurt no living thing:
Ladybird, nor butterfly,
Nor moth with dusty wing,
Nor cricket chirping cheerily,
Nor grasshopper so light of leap,
Nor dancing gnat, nor beetle fat,
Nor harmless worms that creep.

–CHRISTINA ROSSETTI

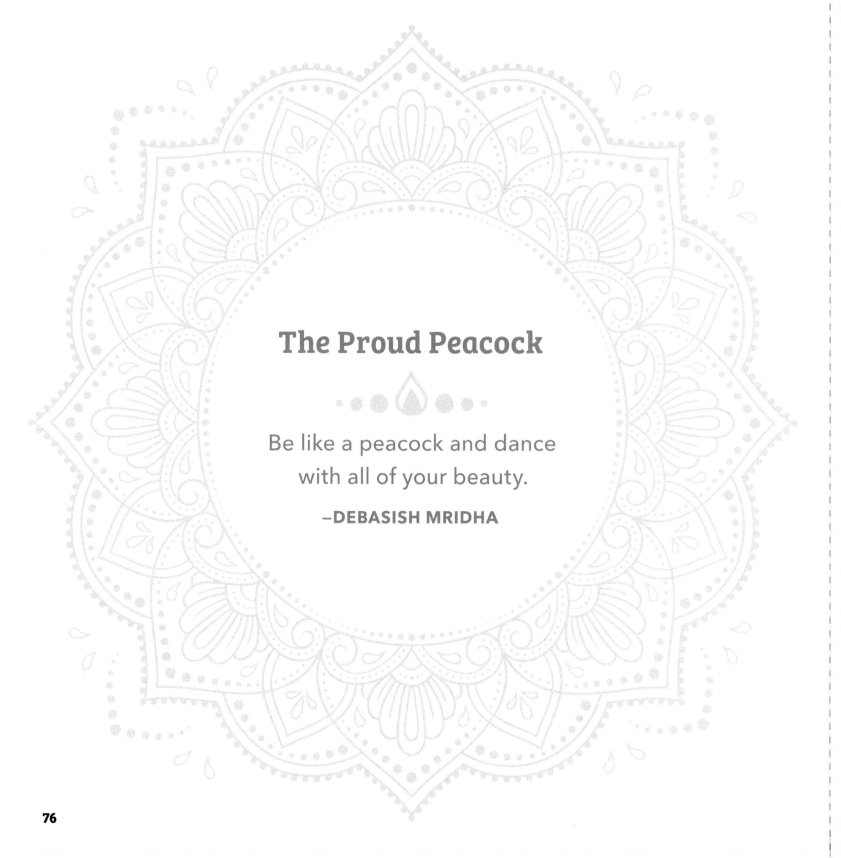

The Proud Peacock

Be like a peacock and dance
with all of your beauty.

—**DEBASISH MRIDHA**

The Treacherous Tiger

Life is a tiger you have to grab by the tail, and if you don't know the nature of the beast, it will eat you up.

–STEPHEN KING

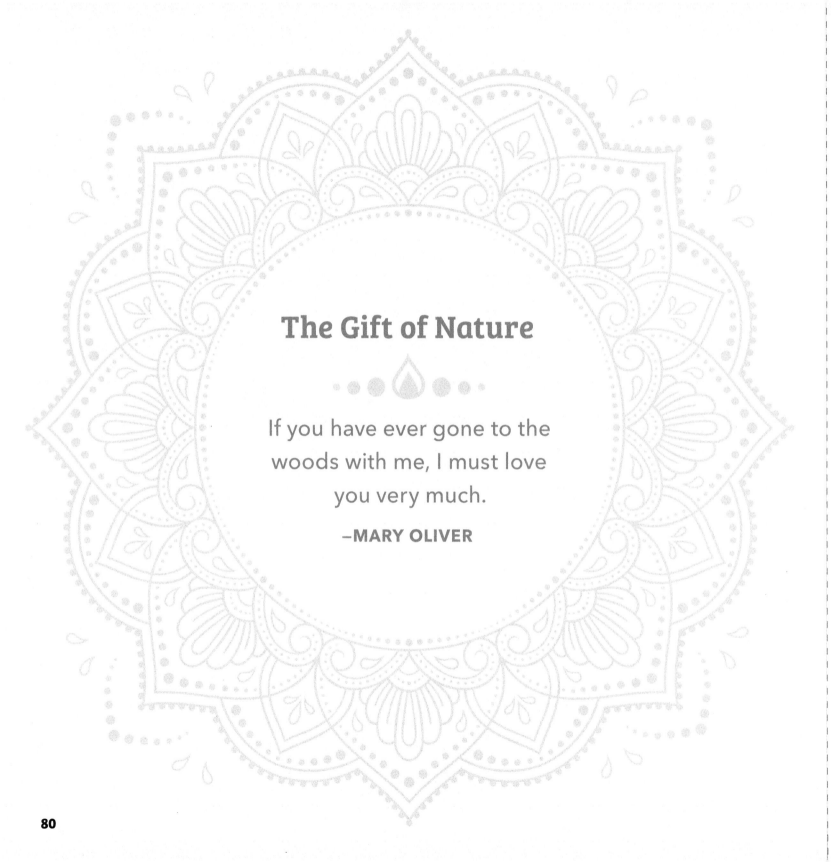

The Gift of Nature

If you have ever gone to the woods with me, I must love you very much.

—MARY OLIVER